Meditations Along the Path

J. David Beaston

Published by J. David Beaston, 2023.

"Experience is something you don't get until just after
you need it."

-Steven Wright

Forward

The image of a path has long been a metaphor for the journey that is life. We can travel for long periods of time in the same direction without so much as a thought to where the path is taking us. When we come to a fork in the road we are suddenly forced to make a decision. Will we go left or right? Assuming we are on an unfamiliar path, (and we must be because this journey is life after all) we can't possibly know the implications of such a simple choice.

All that is and is not available to us in the future is determined by the succession of variables which plays out in each shifting of our weight, each path chosen based on the superficial assessments of a casual glance. As the Alice in Chains song succinctly states "Noone plans to take the path that brings you lower." Never-the-less, many people will find themselves on just such a path, as have I, owing to the human tendency to incline towards comfort, take the easy and well-trodden path and avoid unnecessary conflict both with others and the self.

This book is written for those rare souls who are willing to put forth the effort needed to be sure of their course in life. It is a long and lonely journey, but one well worth the effort.

We'll see you on the path.

Day 1: The power of choice

In daily life there is no shortage of people who do not act as I would have them, or circumstances that do not go as I would prefer. It is not a matter of if, but *when,* I will encounter these challenges that is in question. The true content of my character is revealed by how I act *when* these frustrations crop up. Will I remember that my true purpose is that of service, or will I make the day about myself and what I feel entitled to?

Question for today: The decision is mine to make. What is my choice to be?

Action: When I find myself getting caught up in a feeling of entitlement or frustration I will say, aloud if possible, "This is not about me. How can I contribute?"

Day 2: Expectations and peace of mind

There is an interesting relationship between my expectations and the peace I feel. Whenever the word "should" appears in my vocabulary, it is a sign that there is a disconnect between the world that I am living in, and the world I **think** I am living in. I am telling myself a story that is based on desire rather than fact. Life is a series of inputs and outputs. If the story I have been telling myself were based on facts, I would see that the only possible outcome available to me is the outcome I am currently experiencing. Acceptance of what is lays the groundwork for what could be.

Question for today: What stories am I telling myself today?

Action: I will give myself permission to accept my life as it actually is, even if I am not happy with the results I am seeing today.

Day 3: The source of what is possible

Henry Ford famously said, "Whether you think you can, or you can't, you are usually right." It is a fundamental principle of the Universe that we must be able to envision an outcome if we are to take the actions necessary to achieve it. Whether preparing to run the Boston Marathon, or get a glass of water, all action begins when the possibility first exists in my mind.

Question for today: Do I honestly believe I can be successful? Why?

Action: I will list at least three things that impede my progress. I will also list at least three things that help move me forward.

Day 4: Courage to tell the truth

Wisdom is a hard-won gift. All too often the cost of entry to growth is pain. However, this does not make pain a virtue in and of itself. For most people, pain functions as a sign that something needs to change, but how do we know **what** to change? If my hand is on a hot stove, turning my head won't solve the problem because the pain is not being caused by the direction I am looking. Emotional pain is much the same, and if I avoid making the necessary changes, out of ignorance or fear, I will be acting without achieving the desired outcome.

Question for today: What change am I avoiding because it makes me uncomfortable?

Action: Today I will honestly face the fact that I have been avoiding an uncomfortable truth. I will state it aloud to another person so that I am no longer living alone with this crippling secret.

Day 5: A time for change

When the time has come for change, it is not always obvious. It would be so easy if there were a burning bush, or an angel that appeared with a message from God every time a big change was needed in life. More often than not, the need for change appears as a persistent, nagging desire for things to be different. If something keeps coming up, again and again, over the course of weeks or months, then that is something that has come up again and again, over the course of weeks or months. You may be trying to tell yourself something. Do yourself a favor and listen.

Question for Today: What nagging desire for change have I been ignoring and why?

Action: Spend 10 minutes <u>writing down</u> what life would look like if that particular change were made. Be specific.

Day 6: True compassion for others

There is a small, but important difference between caring for others, and enabling them. The ongoing challenge is to avoid crossing that line. Compassion for others is a virtue that vitalizes human relations and ennobles the spirit, but it can be abused to manipulate some and infantilize others. Compassion must not become an abusive or manipulative vice that feeds or damages the ego. If it does, it fails to be a virtue and instead becomes a pollutant which will poison my relationships by creating an imbalance of responsibility..

Question for Today: Am I using the compassion of others to wring my will out of them? Is my compassion preventing others from experiencing the consequences they need in order to learn personal accountability?

Action: I will give myself permission to say "no," and unapologetically mean it.

J. DAVID BEASTON

Day 7: Obligation to those around me

The desire to see others succeed can sometimes be a burden. I can get so caught up in the lives of those around me that I fail to live for myself. It is a fantastic form of escape because it distracts me from my own uncertainties and inadequacies while allowing me to play at being a martyr. Thus, clothed in an unearned sense of righteousness, I can overlook my part in the direction my life is headed and thereby avoid taking responsibility.

Question for Today: Am I so worried about the choices of others that I am avoiding making choices for myself?

Action: Write down one thing about your life that you are unhappy with. Include the reason for that result. Focus your writing on personal accountability.

Day 8: How I let others control me

There are times in life when it is easier to go with the flow and avoid confrontation than to live authentically and speak the truth. When I choose to go along quietly, I am sacrificing my principles, denying my value, and silencing my own voice. These things are of inestimable value, central to a life of contentment and purpose, and nearly impossible to get back once surrendered.

Question for Today: Am I sacrificing myself for the approval of others? If so, where did I learn that I must do this to myself in order to be okay?

Action: Today I will give myself permission to disagree, without it meaning that I am being disagreeable.

Day 9: The hard work of self-acceptance

For much of my life, I felt isolated from the rest of humanity; alone even in crowded rooms. Today, I make time to connect with myself in quiet, honest moments of reflection before I worry about anything else. To connect with myself is to make myself available to truly connect with others. When I connect deeply with those around me, I can impact them meaningfully by adding my value to the world. Thus, my contribution to the world is proportional to my ability to connect with and accept myself.

Question for Today: Am I taking the time to sit quietly and connect with myself, or am I expecting others to do the hard work of self-acceptance for me?

Action: I will sit quietly for 10 minutes, even through distractions and restlessness, because there is equanimity on the other side.

Day 10: Endings are beginnings

I often fight to avoid major changes in life, having learned early on that change equates to loss and the experience of heartache. This may sometimes be the case, but that doesn't make change bad in and of itself. The pain of loss may be painful, but the loss opens up space in my life for something new. Just as cleaning out the closet makes room for a new outfit, ending a relationship makes room for another, better fitting one as well. Neither clothes, nor people are forever, and for much the same reason. I am learning to accept this truth, and to carry on with the expectation of better things to come.

Question for Today: How am I relying on external circumstances to satisfy my internal needs?

Action: I will write down anything I am currently afraid of losing, and what I think it will mean about me if I do.

Day 11: Forgiving my own ignorance

I have recently encountered a set of circumstances which brought me face to face with the profundity of my past ignorance and defective relationships. Despite my best efforts at self-reflection and personal growth, I have yet to forgive myself for the decisions I wouldn't have made if only I'd known better. Unfortunately, a mistake is too often required to learn life lessons. A child who has not ignored a parent and burned their hand on the stove has no deep, visceral knowledge of the word hot. That same child, one burned, cannot forget and the lesson need not be repeated.

Question for today: Am I harboring unforgiveness towards myself for the imperfect ways in which I have learned to be a better person?

Action: Though I may not like the way I've learned them, I will be grateful for the lessons and the person I can be today as a result.

Day 12: Judging others by our own intentions

When I look at the world and see that it is filled with hostility and mistrust, I am often seeing my own mental and emotional states reflected back at me. It is so easy to disregard the myriad acts of thoughtfulness and compassion I encounter each day, such as someone holding the door or slowing to let me merge in traffic, and instead focus only on the one or two small acts of intolerance or spite I see. By intentionally seeking out and noting examples of human kindness in my day, I can actually change the world I live through alterations in my own perception.

Question for Today: Am I overly focused on those aspects of life I like least? Is this imbalance in my focus creating a hostile world for myself as the result?

Action: When I realize I am ruminating on negative events or possibilities, I will take a step back mentally and intentionally look for something to be grateful for.

Day 13: Strength versus power

Physics defines power as the exertion of force over time. In the social sciences power refers to the ability to reward or punish others for their actions relative to one's own will. I require strength of character, to face the day ahead of me, and to accept it with equanimity whether others do as I would prefer or not. In this context, strength can be thought of as the capacity to continue shouldering the day's burdens despite the inconsistencies and provocations of the world around us.

Question for Today: Am I accessing my inner strength, or attempting to exert power over the world around me?

Action: I will bolster and tap my inner resource, as opposed to baring down on the world around me.

Day 14: The investment of time

Life is a transaction. Every moment of every day I am trading my most finite resource, time, for objects and experiences. We sell our time to companies in exchange for paychecks. We spend our time with those who are important to us. And we get frustrated with people we feel are wasting our time. It is easy for me to fall into a pattern of comfortable lethargy and take my time for granted. When I do, I begin to squander the one thing no human can ever get more of, regardless of wealth or success. My time is precious. I will invest it accordingly.

Question for Today: Am I making choices, or engaging in habitual behaviors? Am I investing my time in the things that are truly important?

Action: I will reorder my activities so as to accomplish one thing that I truly value in place of one thing that I simply do.

Day 15: Sustained meaningful relationships

Relationships come in many forms and not all are created equal. My relationship with my brother is different than that with my boss. Both are different than my relationship with my spouse, kids, neighbors, or a telemarketer. This normal, healthy variation in the nature and quality of relationships crosses the line and becomes unhealthy when I disingenuously cater to what I believe people want me to be rather than showing up authentically. When my goal is to be liked, rather than to be genuine, I forsake and belittle myself for the fickle and fleeting approval of those I may not even truly like in the first place. If I lie, or "massage" the truth in order to win the approval of others I communicate to myself that I am unworthy of love and I ensure that my relationships will remain forever superficial.

Question for Today: Am I more worried about how others perceive me, than about how I perceive myself?

Action: Today I will accept the fact that I may not be for everyone. If others don't like me for who I really am, then their company may not be worth keeping.

Day 16: Practicing loving presence

Impatience and intolerance are the natural outgrowths of an inflated ego. Left to my own devices, I experience a deep sense of entitlement and ingratitude. If I don't make time for meditation and spiritual development early in the day, I rarely find it later. As such days progress, with no clear intent, I find myself more irritated and less inclined to give the benefit of the doubt to others, or myself. Eventually, people are not brothers and sisters whom I encounter along the path, but obstacles to the attainment of self-will and gratification. Once this has happened, I am no longer practicing loving presence, or true union with my fellow humans.

Question for Today: Am I using things and loving people, or loving things and using people? Are my priorities properly aligned?

Action: I will set aside what I think is important and intentionally draw my awareness to the loving presence available to me in each moment. I will do this as many times as it takes to be truly aware of the value of those around me.

Day 17: I am and sometimes that's enough
It is far too easy to get caught up in the many things I hope to accomplish and lose sight of the unique opportunities which present themselves throughout the natural course of each day's events. As I trudge through my to-do list, I can lose track of the innate value of my existence and become dependent on outcomes for my sense of worth. When this happens, I have become a human-doing rather than a human being; I have lost perspective on my value to those around me. Using accomplishments to live up to my perception of others' perceptions of me can never provide the sense of lasting worth I seek and since neither my perception, nor others' are indefatigable or flawless.

Question for Today: What do I think will make me happy today and what can it provide that I don't already possess within?

Action: I will stop what I am doing and sit quietly with the fact of my existence. I will allow myself to settle within before beginning again from a state of clear intention.

Day 18: Permission to grieve

Life is a series of ups and downs that often bring a sense of loss. Seasons change. Relationships begin and end. People are born, grow old, and die. I often find myself attempting to move forward from one stage of life to the next without allowing myself the time I need to fully celebrate wins and grieve losses. No human emotion is without its equal opposite. The depth of my grief is inversely proportional to the heights of my love and to deny myself permission to grieve is to limit my experience of, and capacity for, love.

Question for Today: What judgements and limitations am I placing on my sorrow and how am I limiting my humanity as a result?

Action: I will embrace the fullness of my humanity. I will give myself permission to grieve.

Day 19: Sacrifice must be costly

Love is a verb. Meaningful human relationships require personal self-sacrifice in order to develop fully, and sacrifice, by definition, must be costly. If it doesn't cost me something, then it isn't truly a sacrifice. But sacrifice must also be reciprocal, or it quickly becomes imbalanced, unhealthy, and often abusive. No human being is perfect and therefore, no human relationship is perfect either. It is the measure of my willingness to serve, and be served by, those around me that determines the relative wealth or poverty of my relationships. In order to develop healthy relationships, I must both offer and receive sacrifice.

Question for Today: Am I willing to both give and receive in an act of love today?

Action: Rather than insisting on everything being done my way, I will look for the merit in others' perspectives. I will identify the value in the approach of others, and be willing to do things another way.

Day 20: The importance of self-advocacy

When the time comes for words, I will know what to say. But only if I practice speaking. Self-advocacy is a skill that must be trained and practiced in order to be effective. As much as others may love and care about me, as much as they may want what is best for me, I must be willing to speak for myself to get what I really want and need. If I do not self-advocate, then I am outsourcing my wellbeing and maintaining the circumstances for my own victimhood because even if I get what I want from others, I can lose it to them just as quickly. If I do not routinely practice self-advocacy the entirety of my well being is in the hands of others and I am powerless over my own fate. To choose not to speak up on my own behalf is to choose to be perpetually unhappy.

Question for Today: In what areas am I relying on others to provide me with happiness and what would it look like if I could take care of myself?

Action: Today I will acknowledge, if only to myself, the things I *truly need* from the world around me.

Day 21: It's ok not to be ok

I once knew a girl who lamented what she referred to as her "issues" and wished that she could just be happy the way everyone else seemed to be. She struggled with a painful past, which impeded the forming of meaningful relationships in the present. She struggled to accept that there was nothing wrong with her at all; that her pain and sadness were the only healthy response to her life up to this point. Sometimes pain is the only reasonable response to the circumstances of our lives, and as long as I don't make that pain the whole of my identity, it's ok not to be ok.

Question for Today: Have I given myself permission to be unhappy from time to time, or do I put on the face I believe others want to see?

Action: I will allow myself to be unhappy today if that is how I truly feel. I will not put on a mask for the benefit of others.

Day 22: The need to take a break

Sometimes I am overwhelmed by the responsibilities and expectations of my life. No matter how much I love them, even my pets get on my nerves eventually. That is why I am intentional about making time to be alone and recharge my spirit. I am not denying those around me, but saying yes to myself. After all, I am pretty good company, so I want to spend time with me as well.

Question for Today: Have I made time for myself recently, or am I running myself ragged to meet the expectations of others?

Action: I will make the time for myself, if I truly need it. I will go so far as to schedule time for myself on my calendar to be sure that I follow through on this important commitment to myself.

Day 23: Courage to weather the storm

Just because someone is angry with me does not mean that I am wrong. In the past, I have accepted every criticism and offense taken as evidence of my personal failure. Today I understand that others' reactions and emotional states are as much their responsibility as mine are my responsibility. I act. Others perceive. Others act. I perceive. It may be that I have room to be clearer or more considerate in my communication. I may also have room to be more generous in my interpretation. But I do not accept responsibility for the emotional states or actions of others.

Question for Today: Am I accepting every critique of my actions and character without discernment?

Action: Today I will be courageous enough to consider others' input, without automatically accepting it.

Day 24: The desire to achieve greatly

Throughout my life I have struggled with an incessant desire to pursue extreme achievements. This desire to achieve greatness has motivated me to pursue many laudable goals, but not always for the right reason. When I pursue something because it has inherent meaning and makes me feel more in touch with the deepest and truest part of myself, I am motivated by a healthy and productive drive. However, when my desire to achieve is motivated by a need to prove to others and myself that I am important and have value, the drive is rooted in insecurity. When I am driven thusly, my accomplishments only mask and protect my insecurity, which allows the insecurity to grow.

Question for Today: Am I pursuing an achievement because it is legitimately important to me, or to prove to others that I should be important to them?

Action: I will pause briefly in the midst of my pursuits today and honestly ask myself why.

Day 25: The shifting line of happiness

All too often I find myself listing the things that I must obtain in order to be happy. "When I get a date, then I'll be happy." "When my parents accept me, then I'll be happy," "When I get a raise, then I'll be happy." The unfortunate truth behind these statements is that I am really saying that I can't and won't be happy until I have these things. But if I can't be happy without them, then having them will only distract from my preexisting unhappiness. How many times have I obtained my desires, only to move the goalpost further down-field by identifying something else I feel I am lacking and what are the odds that THIS TIME, I've identified the right external object?

Question for Today: What external circumstance am I blaming for my internal spiritual and emotional condition?

Action: I will accept that no external person or thing can fix what is happening inside. I will recommit to doing the challenging personal work that makes true inner peace possible.

Day 26: The banality of intuitive guidance

I have often delayed action for days or months because I was waiting for inspiration and intuitive guidance. I have also driven myself crazy looking for a sign in every bird, bug, and leaf that I passed. Neither of these approaches have been fruitful in directing me towards proper, productive action because all too often inspiration is the simple, nagging awareness that my bathroom is dirty and my bills are due. There may very well be a burning bush experience somewhere in my future. I will do the dishes while I wait to find out.

Question for Today: Am I failing to make forward progress because I do not feel inspired enough?

Action: I will take the action in front of me and trust that inspiration will follow.

Day 27: A genuine spiritual experience

There is a lot of misunderstanding and suspicion around spiritual terminology these days. People often associate spirituality with a particular religious doctrine, mystics, hippies, or huxters. The simplest definition of spirituality I have heard is those aspects of the human experience which are intangible and/or unquantifiable. Viewed in this way, the experience of calm that attends a deep breath, slowly let out, or the sense of clarity that comes when we consciously take a step back from what we are expecting to happen and engage with what is really going on around us can be conceived of as spiritual. A spiritual experience is simply the experiencing of my human spirit.

Question for Today: Have I been overcomplicating my spiritual journey by demanding far too much?

Action: I will take a step back from my expectations and consciously reconsider the experiencing of my own spiritual nature.

Day 28: The curse of free will

A friend once quietly confided in me regarding the fear and uncertainty surrounding his current path in life. He wasn't sure about the person he was dating, the job he was working, or if he was even living in the right state. He was considering moving and going back to school, but was afraid of the new start and the attendant sacrifices it implied. He was afraid to make a decision because the outcome was uncertain and desperately wanted someone to just tell him what to do. He could not accept the fact that there are no guarantees in life, and it is the very uncertainty he was trying to avoid that makes it an adventure. In short, he was afraid of the consequences of his own free will.

Question for Today: Am I living in fear and avoiding decisions because I don't want to face the responsibility or potential consequences?

Action: I will commit, through action, and begin moving forward towards my goals knowing that I will learn more along the way.

Day 29: Ingratitude for those around me

As a child I held so much resentment for those who had left me, that I failed to appreciate those who had not. My attitude toward those who stayed functioned only to drive them away as well. This loss fostered further resentment, the cycle continued, and my broken, unhealthy relationships became a self-fulfilling prophecy. Today I know that the only constant in each of my relationships is me and while I may not be the *only* factor, I must acknowledge that I do play a part. If I don't acknowledge this, I will remain at the mercy of circumstance. I will remain a spectator, rather than a participant, in my own life and am unlikely to truly appreciate those loyal and constant persons who have stuck with me through it all.

Question for Today: Am I focused on the wrongs I feel have been done to me, or on my reaction to those events?

Action: I will acknowledge my part, however small, and move forward with the knowledge that I have a role to play in my own relationship pattern.

Day 30: Generating forward momentum

Every decision carries with it a small charge of energy which measurably wires the brain. This, in turn, makes that decision easier to choose and act on again in the future. By choosing options such as discipline, self-sacrifice, and fitness, which move me closer to my desired outcomes, I am not just taking a step forward, but slightly accelerating my progress in that area. Unfortunately, avoidance, gluttony, and laziness have the same effect. For this reason, every decision I make accelerates my progress down its particular path so that ultimately, whether I take meaningful, productive actions towards my goals, or not, I am building momentum. The question is simply one of directions.

Question for Today: Am I creating fruitful or unfruitful habits?

www.ingramcontent.com/pod-product-compliance
Lightning Source LLC
Chambersburg PA
CBHW030403160726
47992CB00007B/2936